MY
AFRICAN DO[G]
MTOTO

MY
AFRICAN DO
MTOTO

Glimpses into The Love of Go

CELESTE DAVIS

XULON PRESS

Xulon Press
2301 Lucien Way #415
Maitland, FL 32751
407.339.4217
www.xulonpress.com

Unless otherwise indicated, Scripture quotations taken from the
King James Version (KJV) – *public domain*.

Paperback ISBN-13: 978-1-6628-1409-9
Hardcover ISBN-13: 978-1-6628-1410-5
Ebook ISBN-13: 978-1-6628-1411-2

THIS IS A TRUE STOR

This book is Dedicated to
My Granddaughters
Rachael, Megan, and Hannah
Gretchen, Mia, and Edison
My Great Grandchildren
Brantley and Kasen
Jude, Caleb, and Madison
And those yet to come
and to all the children who have sat on my lap over ~~r~~
in many countries.

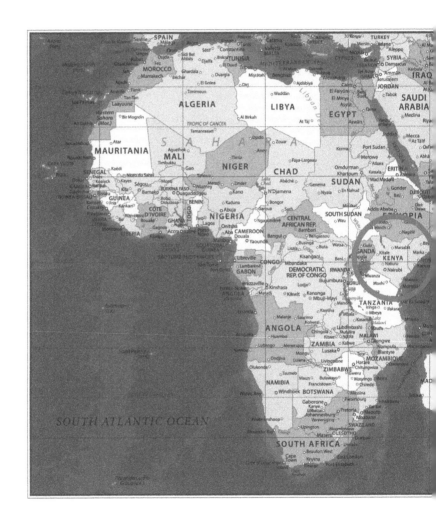

TABLE OF CONTENTS

Chapter One

SOMETHING
OUTSIDE THE CAMP

I awoke with a start! Something was outside th
kept very still, not daring to even breathe. We h
to the Baringo District the day before and barely ma
before the sun began to set. The African night was
but as I gazed out the tent window the stars were a
'*Thank you*' Lord for bringing us here.

There!! I heard it again. Soft sounds of so
moving around! We had seen many goats in the a
scape and had been warned that the hippos from
came out to root for foliage at night. We were not
that far from the lake. Then I heard a soft whimper

ed because it sounded like a newborn puppy. *'I must*
ning' I thought. I certainly was not going outside
in the dead of an African night to find out! *'Too*
s,' I said to myself. After some time, the silence of
t told me I must have been dreaming after all and I
ack into a deep sleep.

Chapter Two

MORNING CHORES

The morning sun shone in my eyes relentlessly. have to get up. Johnston, our cook, and interpr already starting the fire for coffee and I was so gra his assistance.

Benson and David, two other young men we w toring in the Lord, had joined our team for the bu They were chopping wood and hauling water. Every several jobs around the camp and the morning ch begun. Loren, my husband, was already up and c the plane, making sure no one had disturbed it du night. A bush pilot's responsibilities had taken mo attention making sure everything was secure. This

ome true. We were living out our desire to minister
nterior of Africa to unreached people groups!
ten years in East and Central Africa, the Ministry
own plane and could penetrate the deep bush. This
ve could more quickly reach and tell others of The
o loved them and sent His own Son, Jesus Christ to
hem and live with Him forever in Heaven. This was
day in this area and we were excited and anxious to
lay before us.

Chapter Three

UNEXPECTED COMPAN

s I opened the tent flap, a small crowd of faces
from across the way. It seems the village childrer
to see what the *'wazungu,'* (white ones) looked like
we had come. We were to have no privacy after t
morning. Our camp was always filled with many v

Johnston handed me a cup of steaming coff
exchanged morning greetings of *Lala Salama*.
sleep well? I asked, wondering if they had heard any
noises in the night.

Benson immediately went into his tent and came
the scrawniest little thing I had ever seen. It was a p

an a few weeks old that had apparently been sepa-
m its mother. She was wild with hunger.
ere having bread with peanut butter we had brought
rom the city until we could buy eggs and goat milk
: local villagers.
offered the poor thing food, she ate ravenously,
y hands with razor-sharp baby teeth.
to put her down because she was drawing blood
trying to get more food. She downed three peanut
ndwiches before she calmed down and felt satisfied.
: found a bush to hide under and immediately fell
1y heart reached out to her seeing her in this pitiful
n.
oat was so dirty, and you could see her ribs. She was
, not much bigger than my hand.

Chapter Four
A PLACE TO BELONG

How long had she been wandering about and t
survive? Maybe since her birth?

We were in a wilderness and it was a very dry an
land waiting for the soon coming hard rains. T
perature was extremely hot. The only water anywl
the Croc and Hippo infested lake. How had she
up to now?

I turned and greeted the native children and ask
pup belonged to any of them or if they knew where s
from. They smiled shyly as I spoke to them in my
Kiswahili. No one knew anything and they thougl

sly funny that I should try to speak to them in their
ngue!

ughout the morning I kept a close watch on the little
nder the bush. I did not want her wandering away.
ready purposed in my heart to nurse her back to
and then what? I did not know. African dogs had
for themselves.

w the people out here struggled mightily to feed
ves and their own children. We had already observed
digging for roots to eat so there was no hope for a
p in finding a home among these people.

ıld keep her if I could. Then, I would depend on
help me find her a good home.

Chapter Five

A NEW FRIEND

S oon the little puppy woke up and stated to root
I walked over and bent low with food and water
ran from me in fear.

I squatted down and spoke softly, reassuring her
was safe, but again, she ran from me in fear. I caug
her and scooped her up, gently, guiding her nose
hand full of water.

She drank thankfully but was visibly shaking.
softly to her assuring her that she was safe, and that
take care of her needs.

She began to calm down and nestled into my ar
fully. I carried her around inside my blouse the rest o

eart was comforted knowing now that she was
g me, well, the food and water at least, and that she
rvive if I had any say about it!
ening she was running to me for food and after
e would snuggle into my arms beginning to feel
had found a safe place.
night I gave her to Benson to sleep in the tent
men. I knew I was getting attached to her. I had
ol my emotions. If she were to survive I could not
nize' her into one of our pampered pets.
ld nurse her back to life, but she needed to remain
natural instincts to be able survive in Africa.

Chapter Six

MBWA

The next morning, I jumped up with great expect[a...]
I came out of our tent, the little puppy came ru[n...]
greet me wagging her tail and overly excited as she rec[...]
me. My heart was so glad!

As I stooped down to pet her, she began to root in [...]
looking for food. She had remembered that this lady [...]
the day before and she was ready for more.

I called out to Benson to bring me a slice of pean[ut...]
bread (*mkate*) and she ate, devouring every crumb, [...]
might never get any more.

We enjoyed watching her try to get the peanut b[utter...]
her whiskers! Then off she went again under her bush

w I was in serious trouble. This dog (*mbwa*) had cap-
y heart as much as did the people of this dry land!

Chapter Seven

THE TALKING PLANE

The villagers were observing everything in our ca
thought these people were very strange to be tal
of a dog as if it were a child!

It amused them to watch me gently care for this l
ture and yet somehow, they were touched by it. Peo
too hungry and needy themselves to think about c
an animal in this way.

The villagers came and went all day long, staying u
were bored with observing us or until they had so
better to do.

omen would stop in our camp on their way to find firewood. They would linger and watch everything doing until we would speak to them.

s way, we led many to know about the loving God sent His only begotten son Jesus Christ to this earth. n, He made a way for them to live in a beautiful place eaven someday.

ren were always there in groups and it was a play->f activity as they watched us set up our equipment :hing. We were as much a curiosity to them as any-:y had ever seen.

oved the plane. Loren would hook up a long, wide nner to the plane that said, '*MKUTANO INJILI*', "Gospel Meeting".

so used a speaker to announce the ie flew low around the village to call le to gather at the city center. They zed that the flying machine could talk! e came from all over the Region to see vere doing every day. Nothing escaped ious gaze and we always had ad and butter sandwiches for isiting our camp.

They took it all in and told their friends that the
hear about the 'Living God' who knew where they li
They could learn about salvation at the *Wazungu*

Chapter Eight

LOVE EXPRESSED

ghout all this, the puppy flourished. Every day she
d run to my hands looking for her daily bread, and
was filling out and looking healthy. Goat milk had
ded to her diet and eggs too when we had them.

day, in our usual routine of greeting each other in
ning, a curious thing happened. Instead of running
nds as she normally did to find her food, the puppy
jumped into my arms and licked my face!

so happy! She had expressed her love for me above
first!

My heart was so full. I was touched as I began t[...]
that this was every man's story. Lost and helpless, d[...]
hungry, needing a friend, each one of us needs the [...]

As God heard our cries and saw our condit[...]
reached down and took us in. Feeding us, making[...]
our provision, He would gently care for us, even [...]
ran and hid from Him in fear and confusion.

Then the day came when our fears subsided, [...]
decided to trust Him and love Him of our *own ch*[...]

Now I knew what I would call the pup.

I ran over to the team and announced that we w[...]
her *MTOTO.*

This word refers to a baby or a little child in Kis[...]

JESUS SAID, *"Suffer (permit) the little*
children, and forbid them not, to come unto
me; for of such is the kingdom of Heaven".
Matthew 19:14 KJV

WHAT NOW?

is just talking to God.

an come into His *forever family* right now by just

im that you want His son, Jesus Christ, to be your

Tell Him that you are sorry for your sin and that

d his protection and his provision for your life.

m by Faith that His Words are True.

ns 10: 9-10 <u>promises us</u>

ou shalt confess with thy mouth the Lord Jesus,

believe in thine heart that God hath raised Him

dead, thou shalt be saved.

ith the heart man believeth unto righteousness;

the mouth confession is made unto salvation.

v Him in Baptism as a testimony for the remission

Mark 1:4

Welcome to the Family of God
This the just the beginning of the rest of you

AFTERWORD

M TOTO went home with Benson after our to
bush of Kenya. She lives with a wonderful far
loves her in Nakuru in the Great Rift Valley.

SOME SIMPLE
WAHILI VOCABULARY
VORDS IN THIS BOOK

HILI is the National Language of Tanzania and
Kenya East Africa

rs.

 sir or mister

 – food

ani – what is the news (greeting)

jema – the news is good (in reply)

nay I come in?

ɔ (Jambo) – Hello

– Hello (in reply)

 come near (literal) / welcome

Hatari – danger

Lala salaama– Sleep safely or well

Maji – water

Mbwa -dog

Mkate (mikate) – loaf of bread (loaves)

Mtoto (Watoto) – child (children)

Mzungu (wazungu) – Europeans or white ones

Rafiki – friend

Celeste Davis is author of the book,
OUT OF THE FIRE, **The Loren and Celeste Davis Story.**
Amazon .com, celestedavis.org

Other Books:
TERROR AND TESTIMONIES: MY
RWANDA DIARY
MY AFRICAN DOG MTOTO

Coming soon:
MAW MAW at LAKE BARINGO
MY GRACE IS SUFFICIENT (Letters to my far
SUNDAY HUGS
OUCHES of GOLD

She and her late husband Loren Davis were Missic
Evangelists in Africa for 28 years. She continues to
about their life in stories that build faith.

CelesteDavis.org

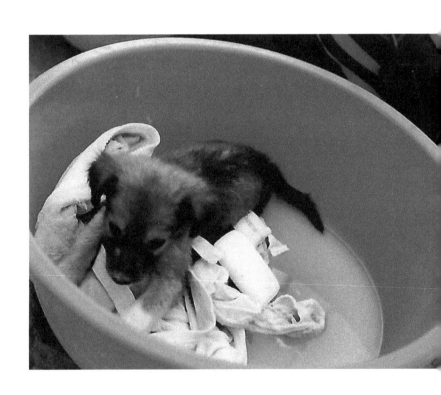

CPSIA information can be obtained
at www.ICGtesting.com
Printed in the USA
LVHW070020260821
696093LV00005B/86